The Election Book:
PEOPLE PICK A
★☆★ PRESIDENT ★☆★

by Tamara Hanneman

SCHOLASTIC INC.
New York Toronto London Auckland Sydney

For the future voters — and future presidents —
of the United States of America

Acknowledgments

Special thanks to Lee Kravitz for his support and encouragement when I was writing this book, to Carol Drisko and Steven Manning for sharing their expertise, and to the people at the *Congressional Quarterly* and Federal Election Commission for their patient and prompt answers to all my questions.

Photo Credits:

Cover photo: FourByFive Inc.
Page 2: Bill Taylor © 1984, Rothco Cartoons.
Page 13: Larrick © 1984, NEA. Reprinted with permission. All rights reserved.
Page 22: Stayskal © 1988, United Media Syndicate. Reprinted with permission. All rights reserved.
Page 35: J.D. Crowe © 1988, Copley News Service. Reprinted with permission. All rights reserved.

Book design and illustration by Laurie McBarnettc.

ISBN 0-590-46414-0

12 11 10 9 8 7 6 5 4 3 2 1

2 3 4 5 6 7/9

Printed in the U.S.A.

40

First Scholastic printing, September 1992

Contents

Preface v

1. Government by the Voters 1
2. The Nation's Top Leader 3
3. Who Can Be President? The Written
   Rules 5
4. Who Can Be President? The Unwritten
   Rules 7
5. Party Power 11
6. Deciding to Run 17
7. The Long Campaign 19
8. Party Conventions 24
9. The Big Show 29
10. What Really Happens on Election Day 32
11. The Electoral College 39
12. The New President and the Next
    President 42

Preface

Every four years, Americans elect a new president. The election is the top story on television news shows and in newspapers nearly every day for a year leading up to the election. Yet most people don't know very much about how the election really works.

Since we have a government of the people, by the people, and for the people, it's important that people — including people like you — know what goes on in an election year. *The Election Book* tells the story. When you read it, you'll know more about choosing a president than most Americans. And although it may be a few years before you can vote, you'll be able to follow the news and understand what is happening today.

1

Government by the Voters

The United States is a democracy. This means that ordinary people decide who runs the government. Every four years Americans get to choose a president, the country's single-most powerful and important leader.

During an election year, all eyes are on the presidential candidates. The candidates are in the headlines and on the evening news. Everywhere you turn, you see a candidate's face on a poster, or name on a bumper sticker.

But the real power during the election is with the people. Each candidate, whether giving a speech, touring a factory, or appearing on television, has just one goal in an election year. That is to get the votes of the people.

The U.S. presidential election is probably the longest and the toughest race in the world to win. And the winner ends up with one of the toughest but most important jobs in the world. This book describes how a few Americans get into the race for president, and how millions of Americans take part in choosing the winner.

(C) BILL TAYLOR - ROTHCO CARTOONS

2
The Nation's Top Leader

When the people choose a president, they are choosing the person who will have the most powerful, prestigious, and difficult job in the country, maybe even in the world. From the Oval Office in the White House, the president carries out awesome responsibilities.

The President's Many Jobs

The president is the chief executive and heads the executive branch of the U.S. government. The president suggests laws to Congress that shape nearly every aspect of our society, from business to education, from housing to health care. He or she is "boss" to the millions of government workers who see that laws are carried out.

As chief of state, the president is the ultimate leader of the American people. He or she must inspire and lead the country through both good times and bad times.

The president is America's top diplomat, meeting

with foreign leaders and deciding what the country's foreign policy will be.

Also commander-in-chief, the president is in charge of all U.S. armed forces — the Army, Navy, Air Force, and Marines.

The President's Top Advisors

To do each of these jobs, the president needs help from many experts in different fields, including international politics, education, economics, agriculture, transportation, and more. The president chooses 13 experts to be in the "Cabinet," his or her top group of advisors. These are people who have the president's deepest trust and highest respect.

When choosing a candidate for president, voters often consider who might be appointed to the Cabinet. They want to choose someone who is capable of doing all of the president's jobs well, and someone who will get the best advice.

3

Who Can Be President?

The Written Rules

If you look at the 40 people who have had the job of president so far, you might think that only white males are allowed in the Oval Office. That's not true. There are very few rules about who can be president.

Who Is Eligible for the Job?

The Constitution, which is the set of rules defining our government, states only that the president must:

- be at least 35 years old.
- have lived in the United States for 14 years.
- be a "natural-born citizen" of the United States. (Basically, that means you have to be born in the United States. Some people say you're also a

"natural-born citizen" if at least one of your parents is a U.S. citizen, but your mother happened to be out of the country when you were born. No one born under these circumstances has ever tried to run for president. When someone does, the government will have to decide whether that person is a "natural-born citizen.")

How Does a Person Get the Job?

The Constitution also describes some surprising things about how a person can get the job of president. The most important day in an election year is the first Tuesday after the first Monday in November. That is Election Day, the day Americans vote for president. But what most people don't know, or what they forget, is that their votes do not directly elect the president. The Constitution says the Electoral College must choose the president.

How the Electoral College Works

The Electoral College is an official group of electors. (In this case, "college" does not mean school or university. College is an official group of decision-makers.) Technically, when people choose a president on Election Day, they are really choosing electors from their state who will vote to choose the next president. The electors vote in mid-December. Today, all electors are expected to vote for the candidate who received the most votes from their state on Election Day.

4

Who Can Be President?

The Unwritten Rules

Obviously, most of the qualities and qualifications that a candidate for president needs are not written in the laws of the land. Neither are many of the steps Americans take in choosing their top leader. There are many "unwritten" rules about who can become president and how they get the job. The American people decide what those rules are and change them slightly each time they elect a president.

In the 200 years since the Constitution was written, the standards by which Americans judge their presidential candidates have evolved and changed. So have the methods used to choose a person for the job. The serious contenders for the presidency know what the people expect from a leader, and they set out to prove they can do the job.

Experience

Candidates need the right kind of experience before people will consider them seriously as a potential president. People from many different professions go on to become presidents, but every president has had experience in government or experience leading a large organization before getting the country's top job.

Since the 1960s, many candidates for president have been governors and/or U.S. senators. Of the 40 previous presidents, 24 have been lawyers. George Washington and many presidents from the 1800s were military leaders before they took over the Oval Office. Six presidents were farmers before they entered politics, and four were teachers.

Courage and Conviction

A candidate for president must be convinced, beyond a doubt, that he or she is the best person for the job. To be president, a person needs powerful ideas about what he or she can do for the country and has to convince people to support these ideas.

During the campaign season, the whole country will judge both the candidates and their ideas. The country watches everything the candidates do. Journalists report on and question every decision candidates make during the campaign, and nearly every decision in their lives previous to the campaign. A candidate has to have courage to face the people's judgment during the campaign and the courage to lead them if he or she is elected.

Energy and Spirit

The campaign for president is long and grueling. Candidates travel all over the United States during the campaign, sometimes visiting five or more states a day. Most candidates for president are spouses and parents, too. They have to be away from their families and friends for weeks at a time. Even if candidates are exhausted and miss their families, they must keep their spirits up and show their best side.

Some people say the American election process is too long and too exhausting for the candidates. Others say that it is a good test to see if a person can withstand the rigors of being president.

Money

Campaigning for president takes lots of money. In 1988, the candidates spent a combined total of more than $500 million while running for president. That's half a billion dollars! To be a real contender, a presidential candidate has to be able to raise tens of millions of dollars from supporters.

Party Favorites

Since 1852, no candidate has won a presidential election without first getting nominated for the job by either the Democratic Party or the Republican Party. These parties are the two major political organizations in the United States.

Political leaders began forming the parties more than 100 years ago as a way of getting many people to support one person for president. Today, the two parties dominate our system of government. Each party has its own system for nominating and supporting a candidate for president. There are other, smaller, political parties, too. During many election years, new parties form to back a presidential candidate. One of the alternate or "third" parties can affect the election by drawing support away from the main parties, but the Democrats and the Republicans have the most power when it comes to electing a president.

5
Party Power

Political parties are an important link between the voters and the candidates. They get many people involved in choosing two main candidates for president. They also organize people to support the main candidates and help clarify the choice people have to make between the two on Election Day.

Most candidates for president begin their political careers by working for one of the two main parties. They often campaign for other candidates before running for office themselves.

Democrat or Republican?

Each party has a platform, or a set of goals it works for. Voters identify themselves as Democrats or Republicans depending on which party's goals they support. Even when voters do not consider themselves a member of either political party, they often vote for one of the party's candidates.

Today, almost all elected officials — from school

board members to city council members to state legislators to governors to members of Congress — are either Democrats or Republicans. On all levels, elected officials from one party work together to achieve the party's goals.

The Democratic Party has been around since 1828. The Democrats are known as the "liberal" party. Today, they have a reputation for standing up for the poor, and for factory workers, farmers, women, and minorities.

The Republican Party has been around since 1854, but calls itself the Grand Old Party, or the GOP. The Republicans are known as the "conservative" party and are sometimes called the "party of prosperity." They have a reputation of looking out for the interests of the more powerful people in America — owners of large businesses and corporations, and wealthy people.

During an election year, the presidential candidates from both parties try to convince voters they are looking out for the interests of everyone.

Party Mascots

Both parties also have mascots, and you will see a lot of them during an election year. The Democrats have the donkey, and the Republicans have the elephant. Strangely enough, both symbols were first used to make fun of the parties, but party leaders managed to turn this to their own advantage.

Andrew Jackson started the Democratic Party in 1828 when he was running for president. Jackson's political foes said he was as stubborn and foolish as a mule. Jackson shrugged off the name-calling and began using drawings of donkeys on his campaign posters. He went on to win the election! Today, you still find the donkey on Democratic campaign posters, buttons, and bumper stickers.

PRESIDENTIAL CAMPAIGNS

© 1984 · THE COLUMBUS DISPATCH / NEA— LARRICK

A political cartoonist in the 1870s began using the elephant to stand for the Republicans, probably because the party was then the largest in the country. The reference was not a compliment, however. The cartoon showed the elephant getting scared off by a donkey in a lion costume! Nevertheless, some people in the party must have liked the image. The elephant became a symbol of the party and marches across the posters, buttons, and other campaign paraphernalia of the Republicans.

The Pick of the Parties

A candidate's first goal is to win the nomination for president from one of the major political parties. To do this, he or she has to win the support of party leaders and voters in every state, one state at a time.

Early in an election year, the major political parties in each state hold either an election called a "primary" or a meeting called a "caucus." The primaries and caucuses let party leaders know who the people support for president. They also determine who will be sent to the party's national convention in the summer. These representatives are called delegates. At the convention, they will vote to choose the party's official nominee for president.

Primaries

A primary is a statewide election open to all members of the major political parties. Some states also have "open primaries" that people can vote in even if they are not a member of either political party. In most states, Republicans and Democrats have their primary elections on the same day. There can be many candidates running for each party's nomination. A voter must pick one candidate from *either* the Republican Party or the Democratic Party. They cannot vote in both primaries.

Although voters usually name a presidential candidate, what they are really doing is choosing delegates to go to the convention. Based on the primary vote totals, party leaders select delegates for the convention. The delegates are expected to represent the wishes expressed by the people's vote in the primary. In some states, people actually vote for the delegates instead of the presidential candidates.

Caucuses

Caucus meetings are like mini-elections in which only active party members can vote. Every state is divided into voting districts and precincts. Caucuses are meetings of all the active party members in a district or precinct. The party members vote for delegates to represent them at the convention, either knowing which candidate a delegate is likely to support or simply trusting in that delegate's judgment.

The state-by-state schedule for primaries and caucuses usually begins in February of an election year. Each week until June, a few states have their primaries or caucuses. During these five months, candidates rush from state to state, campaigning to win both the people's support and the support of the delegates who will attend the national conventions.

6

Deciding to Run

Potential candidates think long and hard before deciding to run for president. They must consider everything described to you so far. Can they expect support from people in their political party *and* from the American voters? Can they raise enough money? Do they have faith and confidence in themselves and in their views on this country? Are they and their families ready to enter the longest, hardest election race in the world?

Years before the election, potential candidates may begin to "test the waters" to see if they have a chance at becoming president. They talk with other powerful people in their political party. They let it be known that they are interested in running for president and try to build support from within the party.

Potential candidates also travel around the country, meeting people, giving speeches, and raising money for a campaign. It is important to see how people react to their ideas. They also want people to begin thinking about them as presidential material.

As the election year draws near, candidates begin

to declare officially that they are running for president. Usually a candidate calls a press conference. In front of television cameras and news reporters, the candidate tells Americans, "I want to be your next president." If the current president wants to be reelected, a press conference is held to announce the decision.

From this point on, candidates are no longer "testing the waters." They are in the race.

The Campaign Team

Candidates for president put together a team of people to help them run for office. A candidate hires a campaign manager to oversee every part of the campaign. Schedulers decide where and when candidates will meet the voters. "Advance people" make sure a candidate's supporters are on hand at each scheduled campaign stop. Press secretaries make sure the news reporters show up. Pollsters survey Americans to see how the candidate is doing. In an election year, dozens of people have full-time jobs helping the candidates.

A president seeking reelection puts together a campaign team, too. A president has many advantages over other candidates in the race. The president is already familiar to Americans. Whenever the president does something even just a little bit interesting, it's on the news. But running for office from the White House is also very demanding. Often there are arguments and tensions between the campaign team and the regular advisors. They both want all of the president's time.

7

The Long Campaign

Usually, campaigning begins months — or even years — before the first primary, particularly by candidates in the party that is not in power at the White House. Raising money, traveling to meet voters, and appearing on television are three main pursuits of the candidates.

The Cash

Almost from the second a person begins thinking about the presidency, he or she begins raising money for a campaign. They ask supporters and friends to donate to their campaign. They hold banquets and have parties to raise money.

The government will also give a candidate "matching funds" to help run a campaign. The candidate receives a certain amount of cash for every dollar raised from supporters. But to qualify for matching funds, the candidate must follow strict rules. For example, a candidate can take no more than $1,000 from an individual.

Running a campaign is incredibly expensive. Candidates have to pay salaries to their staffs. They have to pay travel expenses for both themselves and their staffs. The biggest campaign expense is advertising. A candidate can spend tens of millions of dollars to be seen on television, heard on the radio, and read about in the newspapers.

In 1988, George Bush spent $30,643,977 during his campaign for the Republican presidential nomination. Michael Dukakis spent $28,157,137 to campaign to become the Democrats' first choice.

Meeting People

Candidates travel from state to state, giving speeches and meeting people. They try to tell as many people as they can about how they would make the country better if they were elected president. During the primaries, Democrats are running against Democrats and Republicans against Republicans. So each candidate tries to convince voters that he or she is the party's best hope for beating the other party.

Candidates go to schools, shopping malls, factories, farms, and town hangouts like bowling alleys and cafés. Shaking hands and kissing babies are two time-honored methods candidates use to show that they really care about people. It may sound silly, but wouldn't you like to shake the hand of the next president?

The Tube

No matter how much they travel, candidates can't meet everyone. So, they spend a lot of time trying to get television cameras and news photographers to cover their activities. This leads them to do some pretty silly stunts. Candidates are always marching through factories wearing hard hats or traipsing through farmyards petting the livestock, hoping the press will record them in these unusual settings. And they spend millions on television commercials and newspaper ads in order to promote their image and get their message across to voters.

Debates

A candidate may also agree to debate with other candidates. Debates are one sure-fire way to get on television. They give candidates the chance to let people know their views on important topics. Candidates also have a chance to meet and respond to each other in front of millions of voters.

Opinion Polls

A candidate's pollsters survey Americans to figure out what issues are important to people and what topics the candidate should talk about in speeches. The polls are also a way for the candidate to make the news. If a survey shows the candidate far ahead of his or her opponents in the eyes of American voters, the candidate's press secretary might release the results to reporters and hope it makes headlines. Newspapers and television stations also take their own surveys to find out which candidate the American people like best.

The Field Narrows

Early in the race for president, there can be many candidates for one party's nomination. In February of 1988,

BY STAYSKAL FOR THE TAMPA TRIBUNE

seven men were seeking the Democratic nomination for president, and six were after the Republican nomination!

After the first month of primaries, the field usually begins to narrow. People who don't win at least a few early primaries and caucuses usually drop out of the race. New Hampshire holds the first primary election in the country, and Iowa holds the first caucus. News reporters pay a lot of attention to candidates who win these early races. This media attention can strengthen their campaigns.

In early March there is an important primary day called Super Tuesday. Many states in the South and a few others have primaries or caucuses on this day. A candidate who doesn't do well on Super Tuesday may drop out, too.

8

Party Conventions

The Republican and Democratic parties each have a rowdy summertime meeting called a "convention." This is where their final choice for president is made. By the time of the convention, there are usually only two or three candidates left in the race for each party's nomination. Often, one of those candidates is the clear front-runner for the nomination and has the support of plenty of delegates.

At convention time, all the delegates chosen in primaries and caucuses, and the powerful leaders from each party, gather together. It has to be in a large space in a big city. The conventions often are in sports arenas. In 1992, the Democrats held their convention in New York City at Madison Square Garden. That's where the New York Knicks play. The Republicans met in the Houston Astrodome, where the Houston Astros play baseball and the Houston Oilers play football.

Party members do three important jobs at the conventions: decide on a party platform, nominate a president, and nominate a vice president. It sounds like very official business, and it is. But it is conducted in a circus-like atmosphere.

Conventions are a time for political party members to blow off steam after the primary campaigns, to meet and celebrate, and to show the whole country how spirited, enthusiastic, and confident they are. In short, each party uses this opportunity to make an incredible spectacle of itself.

Conventions last about three days. They open with a round of rousing speeches. Officials from the host city and state give welcoming speeches. Top party officials also speak. Then, a party leader gives the keynote address. This is an especially important speech. It dramatically sets forth the themes the party wants to stress and helps set the tone of the whole convention. As with all major events of the convention, planners try to schedule the keynote address during prime time for the television networks. That's usually around 8 P.M. eastern time. All the major networks broadcast the speech live.

The Platform

The first piece of major business is to adopt a platform. This is a statement of the party's goals and principles. A committee brings a draft of the platform to the convention, and "planks" or ideas are added or changed, until, finally, a majority of delegates vote to accept the platform.

Choosing the Candidate

Next, the convention moves on to the moment everyone has been waiting for: picking the nominee for president of the United States. Delegates from each state have been assigned banks of seats in the convention hall. Many dress in red, white, and blue, wear funny hats, and wave banners and posters for the candidate they support.

Candidates are officially nominated by prominent party members, to the resounding cheers of their supporters. Then, state by state, each bank of delegates is called upon. With a flourish, one delegate will stand and announce the vote of that state's delegates, stating how many delegate votes go to each candidate who is up for nomination. In the first round of voting, the delegates are expected to vote for the candidate they had pledged to support during the party's primaries and caucuses. However, each party also sends delegates to the convention who are officially "uncommitted." They can vote for whomever they wish.

If one candidate gets a majority — or more than half — of the votes, then that candidate is the party's choice. If no candidate gets at least half of the votes, nominations are taken again. A candidate's supporters double their efforts to gain support before a second round of state-by-state balloting. If a candidate still does not get a majority of votes, another round of nominating and balloting is held. This will go on until one candidate wins a majority of the delegate votes and becomes the party's nominee for president.

After the first round of balloting, delegates are no longer bound to vote for the candidate they were pledged to in their state's primary or caucus. They can vote for whomever they think is the best candidate. Party leaders may choose to nominate someone who did not even run in the primaries or caucuses. A convention in which party leaders "draft" a candidate who did not run in the primaries, and get that candidate nominated by the party, is called a "brokered" convention.

Choosing the Vice President

Before any balloting takes place, candidates for the presidency usually announce who they want to run with them for the office of vice president. After the delegates choose a presidential nominee, they vote for the vice president, but balloting this time around is really just a formality. Everyone assumes that the delegates will vote for the candidate the presidential nominee wants as a running mate.

Choosing a vice president is often an opportunity for a presidential candidate to bridge gaps and mend fences with people in the party who do not enthusiastically support him or her. In 1980, Ronald Reagan and George Bush both ran for the Republican nomination for president. They waged an intense fight against each other that had many in the party angry. By asking George Bush to be his running mate, the front-runner Ronald Reagan reunited his party.

Hoopla to the Last

In closing the convention, the candidates for the top two offices in the land give acceptance speeches. Again, convention planners make every effort to schedule the speeches during prime-time television viewing hours, so that as many Americans as possible will see the candidates. The delegates and other people at the convention keep cheering, waving banners, and throwing confetti until the end. They want to show the country how psyched they are to get their candidate into office!

The Big Show

9

After the convention, the field of presidential contenders has been narrowed down to two main party candidates for president. Usually there is a break in the campaigning after the convention, and the candidates don't start going at it again until after Labor Day.

This is not necessarily a calm period for the candidates and their parties. There is a lot of work to be done. If the fight for the nomination has been a bitter one, the candidate tries to reunite his or her party for the big push ahead. There is poll-taking to find out what the voters are thinking. There are meetings with consultants and strategists to refine and polish the candidate's message and plan the campaign. What are the candidate's strengths? What are the opponent's weaknesses? What is the best way to show off both to the voters? What will the campaign slogans be?

Money

During the general election campaign, the government gives each candidate from the two major parties the same amount of money to spend. In 1992, each candidate got $55,200,000.00. When the candidate takes the government's money, they must agree not to spend any more than that. If the candidate doesn't take government money, he or she can spend more.

The Two-Person Race

After Labor Day, campaigning begins again. The candidates resume their hectic travel schedules, again trying to meet as many voters as possible. This time around, candidates spend most of their time in the big states, where most of the voters are, and in states where the contest might be a close one. The big states have the most votes in the Electoral College. The candidates are trying to rack up enough electoral votes to win.

Now that it's a one-on-one fight, a candidate may change his or her approach to the voters. For one thing, the candidate now needs to appeal to all Americans, not just to those within his or her political party. A candidate's speeches and public appearances are designed to appeal to the broadest possible spectrum of American voters.

Getting Out the Vote

The political parties kick into high gear behind their candidate. During election years, political party members are active in nearly every city, town, and neighborhood in the United States.

Volunteers go door to door in their neighborhood, trying to convince people to support their candidate on Election Day. They call people on the phone to gather support. They pass out leaflets, bumper stickers, and buttons with their candidate's name on them.

The party activists try to "get out the vote." They know that many Americans who are eligible to vote often don't. At the presidential election in 1988, only about half of America's eligible voters went to the polls.

Every U.S. citizen over the age of 18 can vote if he or she is registered. You are a citizen if you were born here. You can also become a citizen if you moved here from another country. Registering just means signing up to vote.

The political parties and other organizations, such as the League of Women Voters, try to convince all Americans to vote. They make it easy to register by setting up registration booths at stores, parks, and other public places. They give elderly or disabled people rides to voting places. They baby-sit for young children so that their parents can go to vote.

10

What Really Happens on Election Day

At last, Election Day arrives. The campaigning is over. The frenzy of activity, the speeches, the promises, and the television commercials have all stopped. Traditionally, candidates do not campaign on Election Day. They do what millions of other Americans do. They vote and then watch reports of the election on television.

Americans Go to the Polls

Every neighborhood or precinct has its own voting place, or poll. Usually, voting booths are set up in a public school, a firehouse, or the town hall. It is very likely that voting takes place in your school!

First, each voter must check in and prove he or she is registered to vote in that neighborhood. In some states, voters can register to vote right at the polling place on Election Day.

Then the voter goes into the voting booth. It is a portable metal room about the size of a closet. Inside is a machine that records the voter's choice. A curtain around the machine gives the voter privacy. Everyone gets to vote in secret. No one has to tell anyone who they vote for.

If voters are away from home on Election Day, they can still cast a ballot. They have to get a special form, called an "absentee ballot," and mail it in to the election office in their county.

In most elections, including the presidential elections, voters choose people to fill more than one office. For example, voters will also choose senators, representatives, and a variety of local officials at the same time that they vote for president.

Counting Up the Votes

Local election officials at every voting place make sure things run smoothly and according to law. The officials are usually volunteers from both the Democratic and Republican parties. They record the votes counted by each voting machine and report them to a central election office. Officials from both parties are at the polling places to make sure that all votes are recorded and reported properly.

Some polling places have machines that punch a hole in a cardboard ballot card each time someone votes. At the end of Election Day, the officials take the cards to the central election office. Officials feed the cards into a computer that totals up the holes — or votes — for each candidate, the same way a computer tallies up the correct answers on a "fill in the dot" multiple-choice test.

Some kinds of voting machines tally votes mechanically. Voters push levers next to the name of the candidate they support. Inside the machine there is a counter for each candidate. It looks just like the mileage counter on a car's dashboard. When the election officials open the machine, they write down the number of votes for each candidate on an official form. They take the form to the central election office where votes from all polling places are tallied up.

The most modern kind of voting machine is like a computer. It counts votes electronically. The candidates' names appear on a screen and voters push a button under the name of the candidate they support. The machine sends the vote count over a wire to a data center that tallies votes from many machines.

At each central counting place, officials add up the votes from machines in their area. When officials at a state office add all the totals together, the winner of the election in that state is known!

Prime Time Results

The major television channels begin reporting on the election early in the evening of Election Day. If you were thinking about watching your favorite show on this night, forget about it! All the major networks have their cameras turned on the most exciting show in the country: the presidential election.

As soon as possible, reporters start collecting vote tallies from the central election offices. News organizations also conduct "exit polls." They ask voters leaving the polls who they voted for. They feed these survey results into a computer that calculates who will win the election. Television news reporters announce the results of the exit polls early in the evening. Sometimes, by 9 P.M. eastern time, the news stations predict who the next president will be!

You will notice that television newscasters report vote tallies state-by-state. That's because the state-wide vote totals tell which way the Electoral College will vote and who will be the next president. Reporters focus the most attention on the states with the largest number of electoral votes — California, Florida, Illinois, Michigan, New Jersey, New York, Ohio, Pennsylvania, and Texas — the same states where most candidates spend a lot of their time campaigning.

Prime Time Arguments

Some people say it is not fair to report predictions or state-by-state election results so early. In 1980, early in the evening on Election Day and long before people had finished voting, television news reporters began predicting that Ronald Reagan would beat Jimmy Carter. The results of voting in the eastern states were known, and the networks' own exit polls were showing a clear winner. At 9:45 P.M. in the East, Carter conceded the election. Because there is a three-hour time difference between the East and the West coasts, people in California and other western states heard Carter's announcement at 6:45 P.M. Voters there still had time to go to the polls, but they already knew their vote for president would not make a difference in the election results!

Politicians who were running for other offices in the western states were mad. They believed that many voters did not bother to go to the polls after they learned the results of the presidential race. As a result, these voters did not vote for anyone running for Congress or other offices on the ballot. Critics pointed out that the results of those races may have been influenced by the early announcement in the presidential race.

Surveys taken after the 1980 election also showed that citizens all over the country were upset by the early reporting of election results. Congress even held meetings to see if anything should or could be done to stop the problem. Some people said that the polls should all close at the same time, or that the polls should be open for 24 hours across the country. Others said that laws should stop reporters from broadcasting early election results.

The major television networks promised Congress that they would not report the election results of any state until all votes in that state were counted. But that does not stop them from reporting on the results of exit polls, or from reporting how the eastern states voted before the polls in the West are closed. News reporters say their First Amendment right to free speech allows them to decide when and whether to report on the state vote tallies and exit poll results.

The Loser and the Winner Speak

Unless the election is close, one of the candidates usually admits defeat by 11 P.M., if not sooner. In each candidate's home state, hundreds of supporters have gathered in hotels. At this time, with the cameras rolling, the losing candidate gives a speech congratulating the winner and thanking supporters for all of their hard work. There is usually a lot of crying and booing in the audience. Shortly after, the winner appears in front of his or her party and gives a rousing speech to a shrieking, cheering, jubilant crowd.

Now everyone knows who the next president will be, but there is one more hurdle to jump before the results are official. The votes of the people do not directly elect the president. The Electoral College does.

11
The Electoral College

The Electoral College votes in mid-December. Each state gets as many electors in the Electoral College as they have senators and representatives in Congress, plus the District of Columbia gets three. (Each state legislature decides exactly how electors from that state are chosen.) There are 538 electors in all.

The electors meet at their state capitals. They each write their choice for president on a paper ballot and put it in a locked box. The boxes go to the Capitol Building in Washington, D.C. On January 6, the president of the Senate opens and counts the electoral votes in front of all the members of the House of Representatives and the Senate. A candidate needs a majority, or 270, electoral votes to win.

All electors are expected to vote for the candidate who got the most votes from the people of their state. Some states even have laws that require electors to vote this way. It's a "winner-take-all" system. For example, California is a very big state and has 54 electors in the Electoral College. The candidate who wins the most votes from the people of California will get all 54 of California's electoral votes — even if the people's vote count was very close.

In very rare cases, one or a few electors have voted for a candidate who did not win in their state. They are called the "faithless electors." These electors have cast their votes as a protest. They have never intended to or succeeded in changing the outcome of an election.

Usually, the Electoral College votes, and then the votes are counted without people taking much notice. Newspapers and television stations report the events in passing.

Ties and Three-Way Races

If no candidate gets a majority of the votes in the Electoral College, then the House of Representatives decides who the winner is. This can happen if there is a tie or if there are three candidates in the race and none of them gets more than half of the electoral vote. Each state can cast just one vote. To be elected president by the House, a candidate has to get 26 votes.

If no vice-presidential candidate gets a majority of votes in the Electoral College, then the Senate chooses between the two candidates with the most votes. In this case, each Senator gets one vote.

Only two presidential elections have been decided by the House of Representatives. Thomas Jefferson won in the House in 1800, and John Quincy Adams in 1824.

Electoral Controversies

It is possible for a candidate to win the most votes from the people in the November election, but lose the race in the Electoral College! This can happen if the candidate loses in big electoral states by a very small number of votes, but wins in small electoral states by a very large number of votes.

In the 1800s, three candidates lost in the general election, but won the presidency after the Electoral College voted. In 1824, Andrew Jackson won the most votes in the general election, but the Electoral College chose John Quincy Adams for president. In 1876, Samuel Tilden won the general election, but some votes were contested and there were charges of fraud. A special commission was set up to choose the president. After months of debate, the commission chose Tilden's opponent, Rutherford B. Hayes. In 1888, Grover Cleveland got the most popular votes, but Benjamin Harrison won in the Electoral College and became president.

Today, some people think that the Electoral College should be abolished. They think a direct election by the U.S. people would be more democratic. But changing the system would mean amending the Constitution, and such an amendment has never gotten enough support to become the law of the land.

12

The New President and the Next President

Almost immediately after the election is over, the losing party starts planning for next time. The search is on for a likely candidate. Presidential "wannabes" start putting out the word that they are interested in the job.

On January 20, after Election Day, the winner of the presidential election stands before the Chief Justice of the United States and takes the Oath of Office. At that moment, the winner of the toughest race to run becomes president of the United States.